thank you

THE PATH OF ACCEPTANCE & GRATITUDE

noah cicero

THOUGHT CATALOG Books

THOUGHTCATALOG.COM

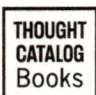

THOUGHT CATALOG Books

Copyright © 2024 Noah Cicero.

All rights reserved. No part of this book may be reproduced or transmitted in any form or any means, electronic or mechanical, without prior written consent and permission from Thought Catalog.

Published by Thought Catalog Books, an imprint of Thought Catalog, a digital magazine owned and operated by The Thought & Expression Co. Inc., an independent media organization founded in 2010 and based in the United States of America. For stocking inquiries, contact stockists@shopcatalog.com.

Produced by Chris Lavergne and Noelle Beams
Art direction and design by KJ Parish
Circulation management by Isidoros Karamitopoulos

thoughtcatalog.com | shopcatalog.com

First Edition, Limited Edition Print
Printed internationally by Amazon Print Services.

ISBN 978-1-965820-00-1

Preface

On June 16, 2004, my brother killed himself. It was one of the worst days of my life. It led me to thinking a lot about why one chooses to stay alive. He was only thirty-years-old and he said goodbye to everything: family and friends, sunrises and sunsets, forests, deserts, movies, music, to all the creatures of the Earth, vacations, ambition, work, having a family of his own. He walked away from the whole universe.

Confronting his death helped me to open my eyes. It showed me that life is full of beauty and if I let myself, I could appreciate it. The goal of my life became a search for appreciation. I was overwhelmed with a desire to experience all that life had to offer. I did not care if the experience was comfortable, *I wanted to appreciate everything*.

When we are children, we love the world. Meeting a small frog is a great joy. Playing in mud is as great as a trip to South America. Riding bicycles down a lonely side street brings immense happiness. Walking through the woods, seeing fallen trees, a deer, vines hanging from limbs, and the green leaves, fills a child with wonder. A child is overwhelmed by the beauty of the world. The whole world glistens for them.

Then, we grow up and learn the ways of the world. We become fixated on what is viewed as "valuable" by society. Instead of being captivated by frogs and owls or being completely content with a walk through a forest and a bike ride with friends, we are taught that those simple things are childish and we should want more. We are taught that we should seek approval from others instead of seeking our own divine authenticity in life. Instead of finding ourselves, we spend our time trying to figure out how to make people we do not even know approve of us. We become addicted to titles and owning things.

But, when we become fixated on approval from others, *we no longer feel gratitude*. Instead of looking at what is around us, and feeling gratitude, we do things because we assume other people will notice.

So, the time has come to let go of this warped mental state of anxiety and wake up from your fixation. You have been fixated on *attaining* and not on *having*.

Go look at a rock, enjoy music, spend time with a friend, laugh with everyone. Yes, *laugh with everyone*. Walk into a forest and touch a tree. Put your palm on the trunk, feel the bark beneath your fingers. Spend time with your loved ones and enjoy them for who they are. Kiss your lover. Hold them tightly. Break free from the agonies of life together. Put your hands into the air and embrace the beauty.

Walk away from those mental confinements, and embrace this world for what it is. Stop trying to make the world conform to your mind, let yourself conform to the world. The world is full of beauty, charm and wonder. Go forth, play, unconditionally love, embrace life, and be curious like a child.

*Life becomes a lot easier to bear when
you stop expecting perfection.*

For those who have become lost; for those whose direction is not clear—believe in your creativity. Believe in your inherent beauty. You are not just made of stardust—*you are the stars*. You are one with our universe and it has not forgotten you. We are all on adventures of the most divine importance so, *believe in your great life*. You have a mission to fulfill.

You matter.

Sometimes I have these painful feelings
that I have wasted my life;
that it is all out of my control in this fast-
paced world that never lets up.

Don't we all feel this terrible smallness?
This overwhelming sense that our
voice, dignity, hopes, dreams,

                    matter to no one?

The weight of years bearing down
on us, making us desperate
for a solid life; for someone to reach out
and give us a reason to live,
to keep going, beyond our miseries.

Wearing our self-loathing like tattoos on our bodies.
Feeling trapped and lost.
Feeling that loving sincerely is actually very stressful.
We hold this great sadness
over a world that always seems to be in a state of crisis.
We want the world to be a better place so
with muscles strained and tears in our eyes,

                    we keep going.

Even though we feel terribly small in this world,

                    we keep going.

A lot of us feel invisible.
Regardless,
you are still important
to your friends and family;
to your community.
You are so important
and will have a meaningful life.

Embrace this world
for what it is.

Let's pull you out of this feeling—this unimportance
—this sense that life is too big for you
—this distrust of the people around you.
Let's validate your life—help you to remember
that beauty, truth, harmony, compassion, peace
is found everywhere—that you are vital and
important—that your life is worth living.

Because there is no end to life's problems,
but this is a struggle *we all know*.

Which is why we have each other—to mentor
—to guide—to lighten the load of being alive.
Which is why we have music—to soothe
us—to dance to—to remind us we are alive.
Which is why we have sports—to cheer for
—to play in—to remind us we can move.

Let's make these the final days of letting
those emotions slowly kill you for you have
so much to give. Your capacity for *being*
happy and *giving* happiness is infinite.

Do you want to be a person who focuses
on what you don't have or,
a person who focuses on what you do
have and what can be done with it?
All of this comparison drives you crazy.
Always accusing yourself of not being 'good enough.'
But you have been through a *million* things in life.
Your life is *vibrant* and deserves *dignity and respect.*

You are allowed to have your life.

You have control over your story so,
let those terrible moments become your strength.
Wrestle with darkness until you become victorious.
You are the greatest story.
You are the greatest wisdom.
Just listen to the happiest part of yourself;
to the beautiful person inside you who wants to live.
Commit to this love within that has
no beginning, middle, or end.
Forgive yourself while you still have time because
the world needs you.
Be anchored in happiness.
It is a decision you have to make.

Empathy starts with yourself.
Honesty starts with yourself.
Love starts with yourself.

You are too important to hate.
Instead, *bring your big light into this world.*
While at times it feels like you are alone; that no one
notices how much to struggle to make things work;
that everyone is taking you for granted; know that
you are too important to let your light be muddled.
And while it's not easy to put yourself into this world
because it makes you vulnerable;
because it makes you question whether or not
you matter. Know that
you are still important and can contribute to this world.
You have gifts and experiences to share.
You have beauty to put out into this world.
And despite everything, the world will thank you for it.

The meanness of the world never ends;
extending in all directions.
Meanness leads us to be protective; focused
on our self-preservation; building walls
to avoid getting hurt. But
the memories of hurt never disappear, meaning
you cannot *fix your pain*, only your
reaction to the pain. So,
sit with your pain. Take long walks with your
pain. Become friends with your pain.
This is the path to peace
because a lot of people still need *you*.
Of course, protect yourself from toxic people
but do not let them destroy the best parts of yourself.
Do not let them hinder you from seeing
the importance of others; their
outstanding beauty; their brilliance.
Remain open to the variety of humans. *Look at us.*
Are we not beautiful with all of our different
shapes, shades, fashions, hairdos, ages?
Look deeper—
                    at the unseen scars, sufferings, betrayals,
                        and the courage to keep on going.
Look at our power. See our gold.
We are all important so
love regardless; assist regardless; forgive regardless.
Be the one that looks. Be the one that loves.

How do we love?

You recognize love is boundless.
You make love a practice, a lifelong worship,
and endless ritual—not a goal.
You take on the responsibility of love.
You let your lover know that you are serious;
that their love is a major event in your life.
You let your lover know that their love
creates a better life for you.
You share your sunlight with them.
You study them—their failures, what makes
them happy, what makes them vulnerable.
You take time to learn how their mind works.
In turn, you let them know who you are.
You let yourself break in front of
them; reveal yourself wholly.
You become vulnerable.
You kiss them and kiss them and
never stop kissing them.
You let them grow and change, in fact,
you endorse their changes.
You have no resistance to who they are.
You share with each other, the wildness in your hearts.
Together, you become artists; making your
world; curating the most tender
moments.

How do we love?

We overcome the past. Yes, you have been hurt. You have invested your heart and have it fall apart. But you are too important to dwell on these failures. You are truly a gift to this world. You can and you will be vital to another person. So make love your career. Practice love. Train your skills in the art of loving someone. To spend time with someone you adore and who adores you is precious and you have the power to create this little world of love. You have this gift.

Your time is the greatest
gift you can give anyone.

Imagine the world through the eyes of a child:

There are plants and animals everywhere and they have their own shapes and lives. There is a moon. There is a sun. There are canyons, mountains, meadows, oceans, creatures. There is love and compassion. There are billions of people and they are all amazing and live these complex little lives. All of these things are happening, making this world. This world. This wild place to be.

Learn how to enjoy it, this world. Learn how to celebrate the mundane. How to make happiness. How to give into radical love, become strong, and feel deeply the beauty of this universe. How to stand up, regardless of how bad it hurts and let the light pour out of you. Become a new person that sees the world through these eyes. A new person that meditates on this radical love, lets it work within you, and lets it make you stronger.

We still have to persist.
We still have to hope.
There is no escaping the dark
feelings. Learn now, that there is no hiding
from your demons. Walk the long path
of life with your demons,
and do your best to create angels.
Taking your own path in life is terrifying,
but you will become the strongest
version of yourself. You can succeed in becoming
yourself because you are strong. Because
your life is not a waste. Because
you are important enough to make angels in this world.

You are allowed to dream
of a softer world.

Do not be afraid of your later years.
Every life has seasons.
We cannot stop our bodies from becoming
more and more. Look back and remember
your youth—making love until the sun rose,
all-nighters with friends, feeling entirely unstoppable.
But do not fear that the summer of your life is over.
Do not fear that your autumn has
begun. Every year is a chance
for newness. Every year of life is
a meaningful celebration
containing so many possibilities.
Do not throw it away.
We must remain open, listening,
encouraging. We must live
full of love at all times. We must wake up every day
ready for the chaos; ready to be strong but vulnerable,
hard but soft, direct but still listening,
decisive but open to new ideas. You are allowed to look
back. You are allowed to understand your life. But
do not be afraid of what's to come.

How to be a friend:

Take a strong interest in them.
Have patience.
Ask what they need. Help them with it.
Be loving and compassionate.
Take time for them.
Be a person they love being around. Be a friendly face.
Have a sense of warmth and tenderness.
Be gentle. Forgive their mistakes.
Remind them "It's okay. We can fix this."
Say nice things. Smile.
Practice letting go.
Be their friend.
Let them talk. Listen.
Help them grow slowly.
Remind them that you love them.

Being a friend is a lovely gift.
Friends do not come easily.

At times it feels like a whole day is
being squeezed into a second, but
know the bigger picture.
Have patience. Let there be problems.
You have struggled through so
many difficulties in life, but
there is enough time to start over.
Life is constantly providing mistakes;
mistakes never end. So practice
forgiveness for all of them.
Practice forgiving as quickly as possible
so you can keep this world moving.
So you can remember your endless potential.
Remember your childlike sense of wonder–?
Your curiosity? The part of you that
inspired you to climb trees
and draw pictures? Never forget your sense of wonder.
Have patience. Let there be problems, and then create
new ways of doing things better. Imagine new worlds.
There is enough time to start over.

You can change lives.
People want to feel that they are essential
to the workings of this world
and *you* have the ability to show them the deepest love
> to talk with them freely
> to make jokes together
> to give them advice
> and respect their opinions
> to be in their presence
> to become so sensitive to them
> to celebrate their life
> to ask about them
> and to ask if you can help
> to make them feel secure
> to inspire their creativity
> to make them feel a part of something.

Imagine the effect you could have.
There is glory in talking with people; building rapport.
Understanding them and letting them
understand you—mind, heart, and soul.
There is so much significance in
creating harmony in this world
And you have the ability to spread love
with as many people as you can;
to give, share, and participate in the
lives of the people around you;
to create a deeper peace in the world by doing so.
You can change lives.

There are so many paths in life.

Have you considered being beautiful? Choosing the path of love, a bringer of joy into this world, celebrating the life around you? You are allowed to leave the prison of toughness. Just walk out. Open the door, there is not even a lock on it. Close the door and reach out a soft hand, choosing the new path in front of you.

Have the courage to show yourself to the world.

You are too important to hide away.
Join the world. The world wants you here.
Become a helper.
Take the time to learn. (You can still learn new things!)
Let yourself be guided to new horizons.
Try hard.
Practice love.
Remember that it takes hard work to succeed.
It takes practice and determination so,
have patience.
Know the value of hard work.
Become strong and confident.
Show up.
Understand the business of taking care
of other people. (They need you.)
Be creative.
Take time to make your art.
Show the world that you can make beautiful things.
Just go—enjoy!
Participate in the lives of the people
who are around you.
Look and become inspired.
Share your talents.
Be like a child—able to keep trying.
Remember that success can be achieved with grit.
You are not a creature born without reason.
The world needs you here. Do not give up on yourself.

Let in your softer emotions.

There is something beautiful about a person. Listen to their voice. Learn about them and what they are thinking. Give them the respect they deserve. Give them hope. Give them a piece of yourself. Know that you are here to inspire, teach, help others to remember, forget, and be born again. Everyone wants a peaceful place to share in the beauty of life and you have the power to create that. Be a smiling friend. Remind them that their life has meaning; that they have a purpose to fulfill. People need that. Remind them that we are part of a community. Remind them that we are not one but many. People need that and they need *you* to remind them.

Treat everyone as important.

Experience people and let them experience you.

You are sharing the world with them.

Don't put people in boxes. You are stronger than that.

Instead, be welcoming; ask questions.

Be gentle and forgiving.

You and every person alive is unique.

Everyone is an individual.

Everyone is weird and quirky with

different life stories and experiences.

Let people be who they are.

Be in the moment with them. Experience the moment.

Let yourself and everyone else be unique and beautiful.

Life is more exciting, wild, and vibrant

when you let other people into your life *as they are.*

Beauty is gained through having everyone involved,

because when people can be involved

with a sense of purpose,

love flourishes.

Trust is the most expensive thing in this world.
Value it.

Practice forgiveness.
When bad things happen to you,
be strong enough to let the bad things end there,
and keep spreading love and hope.
People who ride horses
have been thrown off their horses many times
and still love them.
We all have the capability to love and be caring;
to be tender and *forgive.*

You are not alone in this world.
You are not isolated.
Everyone you meet wants to love you.
Let them.

Ask yourself:

how many gives do you have as opposed to needs?

- Are you constantly needing people to pay attention to you, validate you, placate you, comfort you, listen to you complain, let you control them, have them boost your self-confidence?

- Do you feel angry over the slightest inconvenience?

- Do you feel mad that others do not have to suffer like you did?

- Do you hold grudges?

- Do you bring all conversations back to yourself?

OR

- Can you open up and listen, pay attention to people, anticipate their needs, listen to a person talk about their problems instead of telling them they are wrong?

- Do you dream of a better world, where people do not have to suffer like you have?

- Are you confident that your life means something, that your mission on Earth is viable and beautiful, that you spread love and confidence with everyone you meet?

- Do you feel pained by what others have done to you, but forgive anyway?

- Do you welcome discomfort?

- Are you excited to give a piece of yourself to others, even if they may not have "earned" it, and never thank you?

Do you have more gives than needs?

"Just believe in yourself. Even if you don't, pretend
that you do, and at some point, you will."
—*Venus Williams*

There is a deep joy in believing in oneself.
Life contains many journeys, many missions.
As long as you are alive, you are never done.
As long as you are alive, troubles are
coming and happiness is coming.
Trust in the uncertainty of life,
embrace the impossibility
of knowing the future. Live each moment
as a powerful act of creativity and strength.
Find the joy and celebration in any and all moments.
Find your drive, your will, your ability to make
music out of this mess of a world.
Become strong; a fierce and unstoppable person.
Give up on these ideas of not being good enough,
not being worth it, and not being
as powerful as other people.
This is your life; it is too short to not be confident.

Practice standing straight up. Practice
walking with a firm stride.
Practice holding eye contact.
We have to be tough sometimes to live in this world.
It is hard at times. You have had one
setback after another, but
no one can set limits on you but yourself.
Break free of habits that are holding you back.
Life is long. We may lose faith in
ourselves several times.
But, in these moments of catastrophe, *invent the future.*
Come to terms with your situation,
and believe in your ability to
start a new journey.

Meaning is everywhere
(*if only you want to embrace it*).

Forget yourself.
Let go of your demands
for superiority and
your need for approval.
Share your time, things,
and money with others.
Wake up knowing
that you are going into the world,
and you are making
a beautiful difference
in other people's lives.
Every day of your life
is a process of becoming.
Every day is a chance
to make a wonderful today
and a better tomorrow.
Provide love to others—
an all-around love that never ends.
Life seems aggressively isolating at times.
We feel lonely. The feeling
of being forgotten floods into us.
This world is big and we feel
like we have no control.
But a loving friend can remind us
that there is still love in this big world
and that can be enough to manage
the troubles of life.
You can be that friend.
So, give cheerfully in life.

Create a world of love.
Be the friend that provides
comfort and concern.
Start giving and sharing
because while everything in life
is subject to change,
our ability to give and share
never leaves us. And losing oneself
in the act of sharing
nurtures the spirit of who you are;
grows the love in your heart and soul.
Start giving and sharing
and in a few months time,
you will see how the deepest love
enters your life.

Your reactions are important.

There is no end to life's problems and
you must learn self-control.
You are too important to let the landmines
of life destroy you because:

> Anger will never improve a situation.
> Anger will never make love.
> Anger will not make you friends.
> Anger will never create happiness.

Remember: *you have a choice in every moment.*

Are you going to freak out and make things worse, or
are you going to be strong, help everyone around you,
and get through the situation lovingly and
compassionately?

You can be that person.
> The one that helps.
> The one that offers consolation
> and soothes hurt.
> The one that chooses beauty;
> chooses the path of love.
> The one that others can depend
> on in times of trouble.

There is always freedom to choose.

Someone is out there *right now,*
who will listen to you without judgment.
Your life will be easier
if you are vulnerable, honest,
and willing to tell other people
the feelings you are experiencing.
You can tell someone.
They will listen.

We are often the architects of our own disaster.
We take reality and glue it down,
giving ourselves a label to hide inside.
But you are strong enough
to cut the threads that have trapped you.
You are important enough
to have new experiences and new ideas.
Walk outside into the fresh air and embrace the world.
Just look at it, listen to it, touch
it, taste it, smell it, feel it.
Be open.
You are allowed to be wild in life. To run freely,
constantly learning about and choosing
your true authentic self.
You can change and improve the
quality of your own life.
The sky is the limit for you. The
possibilities are endless.
Try new things, eat new foods, find new hobbies,
talk to new people, travel to places
you've never been before,
consume ideas that scare you.
You can change. It's okay, just enjoy it.
Go embrace the world. Go embrace yourself.
You are too important to let yourself be closed off.

How does one free oneself?
You take yourself seriously.

You are important enough to have peace in your life.

Life brings many uncomfortable situations that we cannot escape from. The most we can do is adjust our attitude to suit the situations we may encounter. Stop expecting comfort and smoothness. Become an agent of creation—someone who can handle the inconvenient, rough spots of life. Of course, you will still feel anger, panic, and other cruel emotions but let them pass through you. It will be up to you to defeat the worst parts of yourself and create happiness in this world. Learning peace is a lifelong commitment; a daily practice that never ends. The great hunt for peace lies within ourselves; examining internally and engaging in making ourselves more peaceful. There is no one path to peace. Everyone is different. But it's important to do what needs to be done. Do the work to find *your* peace. Do it for yourself and for everyone you love and encounter. Find your peace and see just how much light you can bring into this world.

Peace is when you feel okay with just being there.
You have faith that just being on the Earth is okay.

Find your peace.

Recognize the beauty in *every* person.
Recognize the beauty in *every* body.
Look deeper and see the light
that shines in *everyone*.
Enjoy the bodies of this world
like they are The Grand Canyon
or The Rocky Mountains.
Each rock, each body
taking years to form.
Let's recognize the beauty
in all the bodies of this world.

Assert Yourself.

Do not become afraid. You have faced so many challenges. You have many things to say. Recognize the significance of your life. It is not meaningless. Your greatest source of strength is found in your struggles, your failures, your shame, your embarrassments—in the moments when you were down and out *but you stood up* and kept on going. Do not become afraid. Assert yourself. Share your heroic life.

Have the confidence to say, "no."
It is vital in life.

There is no love in being contrarian.
There is no love in telling people
they are wrong all the time.
There is no love in telling people
                    that the music they like is stupid,
                    the food they like is gross,
                    the things they like are horrible.
There is no love in constantly creating a sense
of doubt and unworthiness in others.
You are too important to be contrarian;
it's an emotion unworthy of you.

Be a champion of tenderness.
Be a champion of concern.
This is the path to be cherished.
There is no happiness in hurting.
There is no joy in punishing the vulnerable.
Real happiness that endures
comes from *love*.

There are a lot of people you will not
understand. *Help them regardless.*
There are a lot of people who will never
say thank you. *Help them anyway.*
There are a lot of people who seem lazy
or hopeless. *Help them regardless.*
There are a lot of people who cannot see
outside of themselves. *Help them anyway.*
Regardless of who you encounter, *help them.*

The cruelty of this world will make you resentful
but you must fight against it.
Life requires combat
but do not allow the spirit of anger into your heart.
Fight nonviolently. Show the world your anger
but not hate.
Hate will *never* give you what you want.
The goal of all fighting is to create peace.
So, *do not lose the love in your heart.*

There is a great joy in listening,
>in hearing someone.
>>in holding someone as they tell you their struggles,
>>>>what makes them cry and
>>>>feel vulnerable.

Listening will make you stronger.
So, allow yourself to be an agent of mercy.
Allow yourself to be an agent of compassion.
Allow yourself to be accessible and approachable.
Allow your doors to stay open so that
people can open their hearts to you.
Allow yourself to *listen*.

Spending your life worried that other people do not think you are important is the least important thing you can do with your life. Instead, be humble. Spend your life creating new ways to show love and find peace. Spend your life cherishing the people around you. Spend your life finding joy in every situation. Spend your life committing to openness, mindfulness, and concern. A life spent this way is one of power and importance.

No one wants to hear they were wrong.
No one wants to hear *I told you so*.
Superiority is not the meaning of life.
Superiority will create division
between you and the people you love.
Continue being loving.
Help them regardless.
There is nothing more beautiful in life
than the connections we hold.
Do not lose this beauty
in favor of superiority.

Even if the Earth is a meaningless rock
in the vast emptiness of space,
   life is profoundly serious.
   Our relationships are profoundly serious.
   Our relationships with ourselves
   are profoundly serious.
   Happiness is profoundly serious.
   Love and its beautiful creations
   are profoundly serious.
   Having to get up everyday
   is profoundly serious.
   Who we are and who we want
   to be is profoundly serious.

Do not be afraid to stand on your own two feet.
There is a deep love that guides you.
Let yourself be guided by this love;
                              this compassion;
                              this affection.
A sincere heart can stand on its own.

It's okay to relax.
Let go of the tension inside your body.
Think happy thoughts.
Float away.
You are important enough to relax.
You are important enough to *let go*.

Reveal your enthusiasm.

You are allowed to be enthusiastic.
You are allowed to show excitement.
You are allowed to dance in joy.
You are allowed to raise your hands in triumph.
You are allowed to announce your love.
You are allowed to smile when you are happy.
You are allowed to stop and look at
something you find endearing.
You are allowed to throw your heart into projects.
Let your enthusiasm guide you.
Listen to your spontaneous joy.
Embrace your enthusiasm
and forge a glorious path ahead.

Everyone in this world has their own life experience.
Everyone in this world has their
own specific neurology.
Everyone in this world has different
talents and limitations.
Judging everyone in this world is a waste of time.

It is always better to share
love, not to dismiss it.

There is no shame in surviving.
A lot of us have been through hell
and had to develop grit to make our lives worth living.
But do not feel shame for where you came from—
be proud of your survival.
There is no shame in surviving.

There is still time

to fix all of these things.
You might feel like you will never
get out of this hole. Here,
you have lost all hope. Here,
you have fallen in love with your anger.
But you can walk away
and let the worst parts of yourself die.
Life is long. There is still time
to fix all of these things and
you are too important to live a ruined life.

Forgiveness

Forgiveness is not hugging and making up.
Forgiveness is not promising to
never do something again.
Forgiveness is not spending your life making amends.
Forgiveness is respecting that the situation
could not be managed in a loving way.
Forgiveness is promising to go on with your life.
Forgiveness is promising to let *them*
go on with their life.
Forgiveness is walking away in peace because:
You are too important
to let their disfigured personality torture you
for the rest of your life.

You Are Powerful

"No one can understand a king but a king; therefore, God has made each of us a king in miniature...entrusted with a little kingdom, and charged not to be careless in the administration of it."—Al-Ghazali

To think for a second
that you are weak,
that you are nothing,
that you are unworthy
is completely untrue.
You are important.
You are the king of your own kingdom.

*"He settled comfortably against the wood
and took his suffering as it came,"*
—Ernest Hemingway, *The Old Man and the Sea*

We are all victims of many things in life. There are so many things that we cannot change and it hurts. It's true. And of course it feels horrible. Of course you want to scream, *why me*, until your throat hurts and you have gone mad with anger. But there is no happiness in anger and you are too important to let yourself become the victim. It is okay to announce, *I have suffered*, but do not allow your life to be ruined. You must keep going on regardless. You are too important.

Be Vulnerable, It's Okay

It's okay to break down in tears and tell
someone *I'm really happy you're in my life.*
It's okay to scream when someone hurts you.
It's okay to write sad poems and songs.
It's okay to have feelings.
It's okay to say, *I really love this.*
It's okay to say you have been hurt.
It's okay to say, *I have hope.*
It's okay to open up and believe in the
light at the end of the tunnel.

Our hearts will break a thousand times before we die.
Our parents will break our hearts.
Our friends will break our hearts.
Our partners will break our hearts.
Our managers and coworkers will break our hearts.
There is no end to the breaking of our hearts.

Important people are willing to
show their broken hearts
and let themselves be vulnerable.
Important people are willing to look
into the broken hearts of others.
Here, there is an indescribable power
to make others believe, *you are not alone.*
Feel your feelings.
Give peace to your broken heart.
Help other people live.
You are not alone.

Sometimes the old ways are no longer benefiting us.
We have been living and thinking the
same things for a long time,
but then one day,
our habits no longer work.
Things have become broken.

Do not be afraid to change your ways.

It will be painful, but you have to try.
You are important and can do this.
Embrace the possibility of change in yourself now.
Be open to new habits.
You have many levels of power to achieve.
and this does not have to be the
final version of yourself.
You will have to give life to a new self many times.
So, do not be afraid to change your ways.

You can take chances.

You must understand though that *life is uncertain*.
Chances are never exactly what we want.
And so, it's important to wake up every day
with an open heart,
a sense of compassion,
and a willingness to take risks.
Assert yourself,
stop making excuses
and go.
The paths of our lives are uncertain, but
You are important enough to take chances.

Imagine yourself old. Your body is dying.
Are you cultivating a sincere life where you
do not give into resentment and anger?
A life where you are still laughing and making jokes?
Are you a person that will be full of love even
though your entire life is behind you?

Growing older is not easy.
Asking yourself, *where did all the excitement go?*
You cannot return to your youth,
but you can find a nice place to sit
and watch the world pass by
with our family,
in our community.

Do not be discouraged

over how long it takes to gain peace.
It is said that the Buddha lived
over 500 lives before he achieved
enlightenment.
We are all born into worlds
where resentment, anger, self-importance, and greed
are considered normal.
But do not be discouraged.
Forgive yourself
and forgive those that taught you wrong.
Now is your moment
to stand up, and create your own beautiful life.

Stay alert to the beauty.
Be in the moment.
Be mindful of what is happening.
If you are open and willing
to see it, there can be divine beauty
every day of your life.
Stay alert to the beauty.

Acknowledgements

For their support in the creation of this book, I would like to thank Alina King, Oma Bernice Mullins, Curt Ockenfels, Mallory Smart, Chris Lavergne, and Katee Fletcher.

NOAH CICERO, born in 1980 in a small town in Northeast Ohio, is an internationally recognized writer. His debut book, *The Human War*, was released in 2003 and has since been adapted into a film and translated into multiple languages. Over the years, Noah has published a diverse body of work, including fiction, nonfiction, and poetry, reaching readers around the world. His poetry book, *Bipolar Cowboy*, was shortlisted for the Goodreads Best Poetry Award in 2015.

Noah has spoken about literature in countries such as Peru, Chile, South Korea, and Mexico. Currently residing in Las Vegas, Nevada, Noah can be found hiking in the nearby mountains and desert. He's hiked to the bottom of the Grand Canyon four times.

instagram.com/noah.cicero